My Guide to the

CONSTITUTION

# THE
# LEGISLATIVE
# BRANCH

Rebecca Thatcher Murcia

Mitchell Lane
PUBLISHERS

P.O. Box 196
Hockessin, Delaware 19707

## My Guide to the Constitution

THE BILL OF RIGHTS
THE EXECUTIVE BRANCH
THE JUDICIAL BRANCH
**THE LEGISLATIVE BRANCH**
THE POWER OF THE STATES
THE STORY OF THE CONSTITUTION

**Copyright © 2012 by Mitchell Lane Publishers**

Printing 1 2 3 4 5 6 7 8 9

**PUBLISHER'S NOTE:** The Constitution of the United States appears in the appendix to My Guide to the Constitution: *The Story of the Constitution*. The amendments to the Constitution, including the Bill of Rights, appear in My Guide to the Constitution: *The Bill of Rights*.

The facts on which the story in this book is based have been thoroughly researched. Documentation of such research can be found on page 44. While every possible effort has been made to ensure accuracy, the publisher will not assume liability for damages caused by inaccuracies in the data, and makes no warranty on the accuracy of the information contained herein.

**Library of Congress Cataloging-in-Publication Data**
Murcia, Rebecca Thatcher, 1962-
 The legislative branch / by Rebecca Thatcher Murcia.
   p. cm.—(My guide to the constitution)
 Includes bibliographical references and index.
 ISBN 978-1-58415-942-1 (library bound)
 1. United States. Congress—Juvenile literature.
 2. Legislative power—United States—Juvenile literature. 3. United States—Politics and government—Decision making—Juvenile literature. I. Title.
 JK1025.M84 2011
 328.73—dc22
                                              2011000609

Paperback ISBN: 9781612281841
eBook ISBN: 9781612280868

# CONTENTS

Words in **bold** type can be found in the glossary.

# Chapter 1

# Democracy in Action

Representative Tom Perriello of Virginia was so young when he was elected to the U.S. House of Representatives in 2008 that security guards stopped him when he first passed them to pick up his identification card. Nobody thought that Perriello, 34, a lawyer who had worked in Asia and Africa, would win a seat in Congress. He ran against Virgil Goode, a Republican who had represented the Fifth District of Virginia for twelve years. At the time, many critics of the U.S. Congress were saying it had become a corrupt insiders' club, with members taking money from **lobbyists** and following the wishes of the special interests. Perriello's victory seemed like a boost for democracy.

Perriello said he was writing recommendations for peace in Afghanistan. When he returned home to brief legislators in Washington about his plans, he thought they were more interested in the fighting between political parties in the U.S. than the fighting in foreign countries. He was so disappointed that he decided to run for office in Virginia.

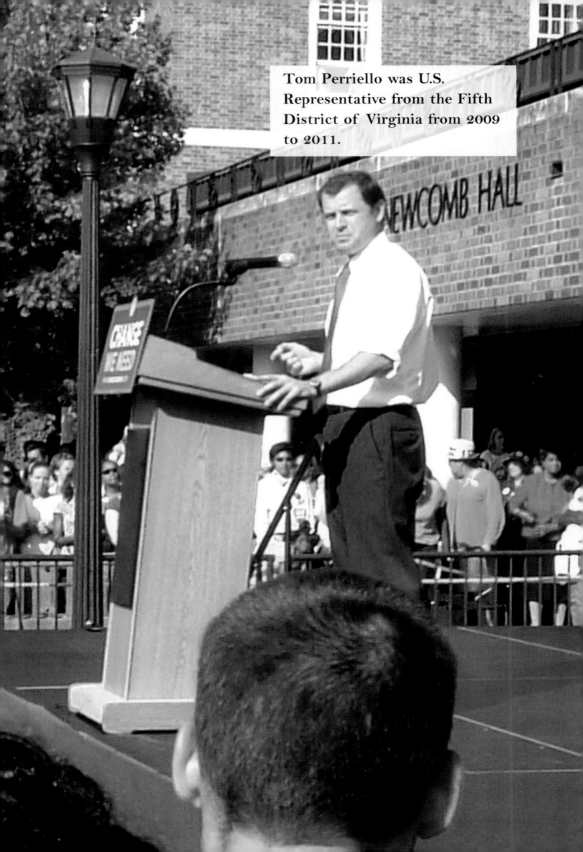

Tom Perriello was U.S. Representative from the Fifth District of Virginia from 2009 to 2011.

An environmental activist, he raised money from hundreds of small donors and campaigned energetically through the Fifth District, which covers a broad area of south and central Virginia. He promised to work hard to improve the economy and support the rights of gun owners.

Perriello was among a group of new representatives with backgrounds in community service. "A number of my colleagues—'newly electeds'—served in the Peace Corps, worked for charter schools and were part of affordable-housing nonprofits. I see that in a lot of the new members," he told *The Washington Post* in 2009. "I call us the Service Generation. What's changed is we've gone from being the community service generation to the public service generation."[1]

While in Congress, Perriello served on the Committee on Transportation and Infrastructure and the Committee on Veterans' Affairs.

President Obama showed his appreciation for Perriello's support by campaigning for him in Virginia. Obama urged support for Democratic candidates for the U.S. House of Representatives and the Senate.

Once in office, Perriello supported another newly elected leader, President Barack Obama. He voted for Obama's health care law and the president's plans to jump-start the sluggish economy.

But Perriello's time as a representative was short-lived. In November 2010, two years after his election, he was swept out of office on a tide of voter anger over President Obama's policies. Robert Hurt, a member of the Virginia House of Delegates, ran against him. Hurt frequently pointed out that Perriello had voted for Obama's health care bill and for a proposed law that would have reduced global warming. The policy,

Coal mining is big business in Virginia and many other states. Perriello supported legislation that would have required energy companies to use more renewable energy and reduce their dependence on burning coal.

which would have cut down on the use of coal for energy, was unpopular in many parts of the United States.

Hurt's victory was part of a wave of victories by Republican candidates for the Senate and the House of Representatives. The Republican Party regained control of the House by a large margin. Although the Senate still had a Democratic majority after the election, some Democratic senators also lost to Republicans.

"We want a renewed opportunity, we want a renewed prosperity, and we want a renewed American dream," Hurt told supporters at a victory rally.[2]

In that election, voters gave power back to the Republican party—the same party from which they had taken it when they elected Obama over Senator John McCain in 2008. It underscored the sort of democratic change and peaceful transfer of power outlined in the U.S. Constitution. Although the country no longer resembles the small collection of newly independent colonies along the east coast of North America that it was in the late 1700s, the institutions that were set up by the Founders have prevailed for more than two centuries. Now, a durable government that peacefully switches power back and forth between political parties seems completely normal and expected. Two hundred years ago, it was not. Indeed, the United States came incredibly close to falling apart right at the beginning.

The political world is full of metaphors. One example is *coattails*, a word that is used when members of a winning presidential candidate's party also win election. Perriello was said to have ridden Barack Obama's coattails to victory. The party of the sitting president also usually loses seats in the House of Representatives during the midterm elections.

Voting remains the backbone of freedom in the United States.

# Chapter 2
# The Birth of the U.S. Congress

After the colonists won the Revolutionary War and made peace with Great Britain in 1783, many of the most important wartime leaders dispersed. George Washington went back to his farm in Virginia. Thomas Jefferson, the author of the Declaration of Independence, was elected to the Virginia House of Delegates and later became governor of the state. The newly independent colonies sent Benjamin Franklin to France to be their official representative there.

The colonies were operating under the Articles of Confederation, a weak system with no power to force the states to work together. Under the Articles of Confederation, there was no judicial system, national tax, or chief executive. The states were imposing taxes on one another, and arguing about how and whether the money borrowed to win the Revolutionary War should be repaid. When Massachusetts raised its taxes, farmers who could not pay them were in danger of losing their land or going to jail. They raised

*The Reception of Benjamin Franklin in France,* created around 1882. Franklin, who served as ambassador to France, was well loved by the people there.

When farmer Daniel Shays returned from fighting in the Revolutionary War without any salary, he was called into debtor's court and faced possible imprisonment. He led a rebellion against the state of Massachusetts. It was one of the factors that prompted the writing of a new Constitution.

a rebellion. Virginia and Maryland were in a dispute over taxes for shipping on the Potomac River and the Chesapeake Bay. Some states repaid their Revolutionary War debts, but others did not.

Hearing about the disarray that followed the successful Revolution, Washington wrote of his disappointment to friends. "Good God! Who, besides a **Tory,** could have foreseen . . . the disorders which have arisen in these states?" he wrote. "What a triumph for our enemies . . . to find that we are incapable of governing ourselves."[1]

Franklin was also concerned that democracy would quickly die in the young American country. "Indeed if it does not do good it must do Harm, as it will show that we have not Wisdom enough among us to govern ourselves; and it will strengthen the opinion of some Political writers that popular Governments cannot long support themselves," he wrote in a letter to Jefferson.[2] By "popular governments," he was speaking of governments run by the people—democracies.

Leaders knew the newly freed states needed a better system of self-governance, but the unity that had prevailed under Washington's leadership was gone. Alexander Hamilton was a brilliant New York lawyer and economist who had served under Washington during the war. He attended a meeting in Annapolis that had been called to discuss trade in the Chesapeake Bay. Hamilton and James Madison, a political philosopher from Virginia, had long been arguing in favor of a stronger national government.

Although they had no success at the Annapolis meeting, they did succeed in calling for another meeting to begin in Philadelphia in May 1787. During a long hot summer there, representatives wrote a new constitution that would create a stronger national government.

Franklin, who had returned from France, was one of the many men present in Philadelphia. Figuring out how to govern the country and yet preserve the states' freedoms seemed impossible. Representatives of the larger states wanted the legislature to reflect their larger populations. The smaller states' spokesmen resisted proposals that would base representation on population size. Another sticking point was slavery. Franklin, a **Quaker,** was opposed to slavery. He wanted the practice **abolished**. Little by little the delegates managed to come up with compromises and agreements. For example, five slaves would count as three people for the purposes of representation.

In just a few pages and under 2,500 words, Article 1 of the proposed Constitution set up the U.S. Congress and divided it into two chambers, the Senate and the House of Representatives. In ten brief sections, the Constitution set forth that a House member would be chosen every two years. He had to be at least 25 years old, a citizen for seven years, and a resident of the state he represents. (In 1787, only men voted and ran for office.) House members would represent 30,000 people. The Constitution gave House members the right to choose their own leader, or speaker.

The Constitution called for two senators from each state, and they would each serve a six-year term. A senator had to be at least 30 years old, a nine-year citizen, and also a resident of the state he represents. The vice president would preside over the Senate.

The original Constitution said each state would decide how its representatives would be elected. It also said that the person who had the second-highest number of votes in the presidential election would be the vice president. These policies and others were changed later with constitutional **amendments**.

Subsequent sections of Article I set forth rules for the Congress, including how leaders would be chosen, that members could not be arrested for minor offenses, and that they could not hold any other office. Section 7 states that all bills regarding taxes must arise in the House of Representatives; it further explains how a bill becomes a law. If a bill passes both the House of Representatives and the Senate, it is sent to the president for his signature. If the president objects to the bill then he can veto it, but approval by two-thirds of the House and the Senate can override the president's veto.

In Section 8, the writers created a list of key responsibilities they envisioned for Congress. The responsibilities include borrowing money, regulating commerce, writing uniform rules for naturalization (citizenship), and coining money and punishing counterfeiters. They also put Congress in charge of setting up a postal system, establishing rules to protect authors' **copyrights** and inventors' patents, establishing lower courts, keeping pirates under control, and developing a national military. The next section lists some actions that Congress is not allowed to undertake. Those actions include suspending **habeas corpus** unless there is an invasion or a rebellion, passing **ex post facto laws** (laws made after the fact, or after the activity was done), and taxing a state's exports. Finally, the list of prohibited activities includes secret spending, conferring titles of nobility, and accepting "any present, **emolument**, office, or Title of any kind whatever from any King, Prince, or foreign state" without the consent of the Congress.[3]

The Constitution states that the House of Representatives will have the sole power to impeach, which means to remove an official from

In June of 1787, members of the Constitutional Convention held closed meetings at Independence Hall in Philadelphia. They planned to amend the Articles of Confederation, but during the meetings they decided to write a new constitution.

office because he or she has committed a serious crime. The Senate, however, functions as the jury and is responsible for handling the trial of any official who is impeached by the House.

The last part of Article 1, Section 10, bans states from coining money, imposing import and export duties, or maintaining armies unless they have "the Consent of the Congress."

Today, many thinkers see the Constitution as a brilliant way to set up a national government. The government created in 1787 has endured for more than two hundred years and led to the creation of the wealthiest nation in the history of the world. However, at the time, it was very controversial. Critics were afraid the new Constitution was setting up a

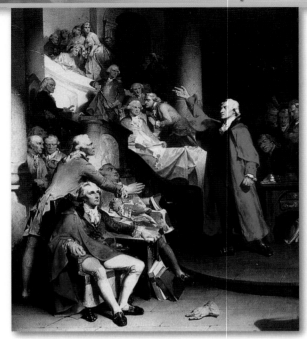

Patrick Henry (right) was a lawyer and governor of Virginia. At first he opposed the new constitution.

new monarchy. One such critic was Patrick Henry, who famously said during the Revolutionary War, "Give me liberty, or give me death." Henry refused to attend the Constitutional Convention because he thought the gathering was leaning toward creating a monarchy. He was even angry about the opening sentence of the preamble to the Constitution. It states: "We the people of the United States, in Order to form a more perfect union, establish Justice, ensure the domestic Tranquility, provide for the common defence, promote the general Welfare, and secure the Blessings of Liberty to ourselves and our Posterity, do ordain and establish this Constitution for the United States of America."

"What right had they to say 'We the people?' . . . Who authorized them to speak the language of We the people, instead of we the states?" Henry asked. "The control given to Congress over the time, place, and manner of holding elections, will totally destroy the end of **suffrage** [will make democratic voting useless]."[4]

When the delegates finished writing the Constitution, they decided that nine of the thirteen original colonies would have to agree to it for it to be **ratified**. The process would allow time for debate between those who approved of setting up a new, powerful national government and those who opposed it.

Hamilton, Madison, and John Jay, who had presided over the Continental Congress after the Revolutionary War, knew they would have to convince New York and Virginia to agree to the Constitution. They wrote articles for several New York newspapers, signing them Publius. The essays explained the thinking behind the new constitution and why it was the best course for the United States' future. The three men were persuasive. The 85 articles have since been gathered into a historic book titled *The Federalist Papers*. Meanwhile, many other writers described their fears for the country's future should the Constitution be ratified. These essays are commonly known as the Antifederalist Papers.

State by state, the Constitution was approved. New Hampshire became the ninth state to ratify on June 22, 1788. Virginia and New York soon followed. *The Federalist Papers* had prevailed.

Henry and others were still concerned about the government having too much power. Madison and other leaders assured them that a Bill of Rights would be added to the Constitution. Madison wrote: ". . . the Constitution ought to be revised, and that the first Congress meeting under it ought to prepare and recommend to the states for ratification the most satisfactory provisions for all essential rights, particularly the rights of conscience in the fullest latitude, the freedom of the press, trials by jury, [and] security against general warrants." [5]

For all of Alexander Hamilton's political and economic brilliance, his death was surprisingly nonsensical. Hamilton agreed to a pistol duel with rival political leader Aaron Burr. Hamilton died from the shooting on July 12, 1804. (His beloved son, Philip, had also died after losing a duel in 1801.) Burr was indicted on murder charges, but his case never went to trial.

# Chapter 3

# The Evolution of Congress

If William Maclay, the first senator from Pennsylvania, could travel forward in time to today, he might be shocked by how much the Congress has changed. During the first few years after the Constitution was ratified, the newly created legislative branch set up the new government, a national bank, paid debts, and planned for a new seat of government on the Potomac. And this was when senators and House members earned $6 a day. This is equal to about $143 today, or less than $18 an hour.

Senator Maclay was deeply involved in those hectic first few years of the government, and his diary is one of the best firsthand accounts of the first Congress. Maclay noted that there was a lot of controversy over whether the government should repay certificates, which were similar to IOUs. The government had given these certificates to private citizens who had loaned money for or fought in the Revolutionary War. Many of these citizens had sold the certificates to **speculators**, and members of

The legislative branch consists of a bicameral, or two-chambered, Congress. One chamber is the Senate, and the other is the House of Representatives. Both bodies meet in the Capitol Building in Washington, D.C.

Congress doubted whether it made sense to reward those who had bought the certificates cheaply.

Alexander Hamilton, however, was deeply committed to forming a strong nation that could borrow money at a good rate of interest if it was necessary. He thought the only way for the new nation to earn such a reputation was to pay what it owed to the certificate holders. Maclay was amazed when Hamilton convinced the Congress to give the certificate holders the full value of the IOUs.

The first Congress also debated slavery, after members of the Society of Friends—also known as Quakers—asked Congress to abolish the practice of owning humans. The Quakers noted that the Declaration of Independence states, "all men are created equal."

But southerners, who depended on slavery for their plantation economy, strongly opposed any discussion of prohibiting slavery. William Loughton Smith of South Carolina said any attempt to make slavery illegal could destroy the unity of the states. "We took each other with our mutual bad habits and respective evils, for better for worse; the northern States adopted us with our slaves, and we adopted them with their Quakers," he said.[1]

Although it did not agree on slavery, the early Congress made other extraordinary accomplishments. Not only did members set up the government, they also approved a Bill of Rights and settled the question of paying the new nation's debts. In a compromise, they would move the capital from Philadelphia to an area next to the Potomac River.

By 2010, rank-and-file House members and senators were earning $174,000 a year. They also had large staffs both in their home district and state and in Washington, D.C. The road from a practically volunteer assembly who could set up a government without electricity, telephones, or rapid transportation to a high-paid body that seems to accomplish much less has been long and winding.

The first major change that transformed the Congress was the creation of parties. At the dismay of the nation's first president, George Washington, political parties were formed very soon after the new

Although he is best known as the first secretary of the treasury and an author of *The Federalist Papers,* Alexander Hamilton was an influential writer and thinker before the Revolutionary War. In 1774, he wrote *A Full Vindication of the Measures of Congress.*

government was in place. Followers of Alexander Hamilton, the new secretary of the treasury, formed the Federalist Party. Hamilton was behind the push to repay the government's debts and to form a national bank.

Other leaders, such as Senator Maclay, were horrified at some of Hamilton's ideas and how easily he could persuade the Congress to follow his lead. "Everything . . . is prearranged by Hamilton and his group of speculators," Maclay wrote in his diary.[2]

Madison and Jefferson decided they needed to form an opposition to the Federalist Party. They called it the Democratic-Republican Party.

In 1796, Jefferson ran for president against Federalist John Adams. Jefferson came in second, earning the position of vice president. During the next presidential election, the electors were tied between Jefferson and Aaron Burr, a long-time New York lawmaker.

The electors gathered and took vote after vote, until finally, many hours later, they chose Jefferson. They realized they needed yet another amendment to the Constitution, the Twelfth, which instructed the electors to choose a president and a vice president.

Although the Founders seem to have envisioned a strong legislature that would direct the activities of the president, that model has slowly changed over the years. For example, President James Polk moved troops into Mexican territory in 1846 without obtaining the approval of Congress. Many other presidents sent U.S. forces into countries without a declaration of war from the legislature. Abraham Lincoln, whose generals successfully battled the southern states in the Civil War, is recognized as one of the best presidents in U.S. history. He was one of many presidents who broadened the power of the presidency. Another was Franklin Delano Roosevelt, who was elected in 1932.

In response to the widespread hunger and unemployment of the Great Depression, Roosevelt created agencies such as the Works Project Administration and the Civilian Conservation Corps. He vastly expanded the power of

Although the people vote in a "popular vote" for the president, an indirect election by the Electoral College determines the presidency. Members of the Electoral College, called electors, are not members of Congress. Article II, Section 1 of the Constitution describes how each state shall choose its electors, and that the number of electors shall equal the number of representatives the state has in Congress.

Franklin Roosevelt was a master speaker who performed very well in formal settings, such as this joint session of Congress. His presidency tested the system of checks and balances between the three branches of government.

the presidency, but at a certain point the Supreme Court found that Roosevelt had overstepped his powers. It ruled that the National Recovery Act violated the constitutional separation of powers between the presidency and the legislature. In response, Roosevelt proposed to add five justices to the Supreme Court, but his own political party refused to back the idea.

Roosevelt nevertheless became a very popular president. He was elected to a third term just as World War II was breaking out, and to a fourth term as World War II was ending. Before Roosevelt, no president had served more than two four-year terms. After Roosevelt, Congress passed the Twenty-second Amendment to the Constitution. This

As a senator, Lyndon Johnson pushed for the passage of the Civil Rights Act of 1957. As president, he signed into law the 1964 Civil Rights Act, which was begun by President John F. Kennedy. People watching in 1964 include Attorney General Robert Kennedy, Senator Hubert Humphrey, First Lady "Lady Bird" Johnson, the Reverend Martin Luther King Jr., FBI Director J. Edgar Hoover, and Speaker of the House John McCormack.

amendment, which was ratified in 1951, limits presidents to two four-year terms.

Power flowed back toward the legislature in the 1950s with the arrival of Lyndon Baines Johnson, a Texas senator who became a very good deal maker and vote counter. Johnson was largely responsible for the Civil Rights Act of 1957, the first major law giving African Americans rights since the Thirteenth, Fourteenth, and Fifteenth amendments were passed right after the Civil War.

However, when Johnson became president in 1963, Congress and the executive branch again tussled over the constitutional right to declare war. Johnson wanted to send soldiers to Vietnam. To persuade the House of Representatives and the Senate to give their approval, he claimed that American troops had been attacked in Vietnam's Gulf of

President Johnson visits a health facility in Vietnam in 1967. He felt strongly that the United States should keep communism from expanding to Vietnam. His determination to fight the war there eventually led to the passage of the War Powers Resolution, which prohibits presidents from escalating conflicts without the approval of Congress.

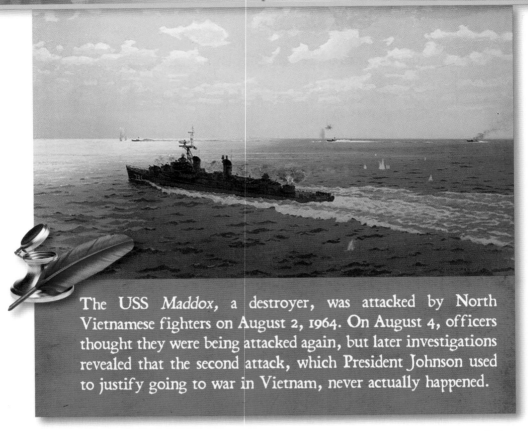

The USS *Maddox*, a destroyer, was attacked by North Vietnamese fighters on August 2, 1964. On August 4, officers thought they were being attacked again, but later investigations revealed that the second attack, which President Johnson used to justify going to war in Vietnam, never actually happened.

Tonkin. Congress passed a resolution supporting the protection of the U.S. armed forces, but never declared war against North Vietnam. The conflict in Vietnam became very unpopular: 70,000 Americans were killed there. Later, investigations showed that Johnson's report on the Gulf of Tonkin was exaggerated.

In 1973, as the Vietnam War was coming to an end, Congress passed the War Powers Resolution. The new law restored limits on the president in declaring war. It states that the president must notify Congress within 48 hours of dispatching U.S. soldiers to a foreign country, and can only keep them there for 60 days without authorization from Congress.

President Ronald Reagan also fell into a huge battle with the legislature when he asked to support the **counterrevolutionary** army in Nicaragua. Members of Congress were opposed to harassing the government of Nicaragua, which overthrew dictator Anastasio Somoza in 1979. They approved a law introduced by U.S. Representative Ed Boland of Massachusetts. It strictly ordered Reagan not to send troops or money to the fighters opposed to the new Nicaraguan government. Reagan and his administration were determined to help the rebels. They secretly sold weapons to Iran and used the profits to provide aid to their friends fighting in Nicaragua. The affair became known as the Iran-Contra scandal.

Congress members investigated, and fourteen members of the Reagan administration were charged with crimes such as lying to Congress and obstructing justice. However, when Reagan's vice president, George H. W. Bush, was president in 1992, he **pardoned** the officials.

## The Committee System

In the early days, the House and the Senate met as entire committees at once. But as the country grew larger and larger, members saw the need for specialized knowledge and standing committees. These committees are in some cases related to how the Constitution assigns particular roles to each house of Congress. For example, since the Senate is responsible for approving treaties, the Senate runs the Foreign Relations Committee. The Constitution also

Legislators have found ways to remain in office that the original Constitution writers probably never imagined. One of the earliest tricks is known as gerrymandering, which was named after Elbridge Gerry, a Massachusetts Congress member whose district looked like a salamander. According to the Constitution, congressional districts are redrawn every ten years to make sure that all representatives' districts are roughly the same size. Political parties have taken advantage of the process to shape districts to include voters who are more likely to elect the party's preferred candidate.

## Senate Committees*

Agriculture, Nutrition, and Forestry

Appropriations

Armed Services

Banking, Housing, and Urban Affairs

Budget

Commerce, Science, and Transportation

Energy and Natural Resources

Environment and Public Works

Finance

Foreign Relations

Health, Education, Labor, and Pensions

Homeland Security and Governmental Affairs

Judiciary

Rules and Administration

Small Business and Entrepreneurship

Veterans' Affairs

Five select committees:

Aging

Ethics

Impeachment

Indian Affairs

Intelligence

## House Committees*

Agriculture

Appropriations

Armed Services

Budget

Education and the Workforce

Ethics

Financial Services

Foreign Affairs

Homeland Security

House Administration

Judiciary

Natural Resources

Oversight and Government Reform

Rules

Science and Technology

Small Business

Transportation and Infrastructure

Veterans' Affairs

Ways and Means

One select committee:

Intelligence

*As of 2011

states that the Senate must give "Advice and Consent" on people the president wants to assign jobs as judges, ambassadors, and heads of federal agencies. The Constitution gives the House of Representatives the responsibility of overseeing taxation, stating in Section 7, "All Bills for raising Revenue shall originate in the House of Representatives." Hence, the House Ways and Means Committee is one of the most important House committees. There are also joint committees, which include members from both the House and the Senate. They include Taxation, Economy, the Library, and Printing.

In addition to the senators and representatives, there is a delegate commissioner from the District of Columbia, plus delegates from Guam, the Virgin Islands, and American Samoa. These representatives can vote on committees, but they do not vote in the full session.

Over the years, several important agencies that serve the Congress have evolved. The Library of Congress is the biggest library in the world. It maintains records of all congressional activities. Part of the Library of Congress is the Congressional Research Service, which provides members with research and legal analysis. The Congressional Budget Office provides the Congress with economic information.

# Chapter 4

# How a Bill Becomes a Law

The Constitution describes how a bill becomes a law in just a few simple words. Any bill that passes the Senate and the House of Representatives goes to the president for approval. The president can either sign it, making it a law, or send it back with his objections. If the chamber where the bill started wants to, it can override the president's objections as long as two-thirds of the members are in favor. If the president does nothing, the bill becomes a law: "If any Bill shall not be returned by the President within ten Days (Sundays excepted) after it shall have been presented to him, the Same shall be a Law," the Constitution states in Article 1, Section 7.

Legislation often follows a winding path from a bill, which is a proposed law, to approval as a law. Take, for example, the bill to outlaw animal cruelty videos. While cruelty to animals has been illegal for decades, people were making horrific videos of small animals being killed and selling them over the Internet. U.S. Representative Elton Gallegly, a

The U.S. Supreme Court under Chief Justice John Roberts declared Gallegly's first law against animal cruelty videos constitutional. As head of the judicial branch, the Supreme Court provides the third foundation in the system of checks and balances within the federal government.

Gallegly attended the University of California and began investing in real estate as a young man. He was very successful and was elected mayor of Simi Valley in California. He has represented the 24th District in California since 1986.

Republican from California, sponsored a law that made selling such animal cruelty videos a crime. A few years later, a man who was convicted of selling dog-fighting videos over the Internet appealed his case.

In 2010, the U.S. Supreme Court threw out Gallegly's law, saying that the law was too broad and did not respect freedom of speech. (The First Amendment to the U.S. Constitution guarantees freedom of speech, religion, and assembly.) Although the Supreme Court's decision was a big disappointment for animal lovers, it is a good example of how the system of checks and balances works. The Constitution is designed to prevent any one of the three branches of government from abusing its power.

Gallegly rewrote his bill, trying to make sure it did not take away anyone's free speech rights. Again it was passed by the House of Representatives. The Senate also approved a version of the law. President Obama signed the bill into law in December 2010.

Meanwhile, animal rights groups were concerned that people were still making money by selling videos of animals being killed in particularly cruel ways. "Violence is not a First Amendment issue; it is a law enforcement issue," Representative Gallegly said in a statement. "Ted Bundy and Ted Kaczynski tortured or killed animals before killing people. The FBI, U.S. Department of Education, and the U.S. Department of Justice consider animal cruelty to be one of the early warning signs of potential violence by youths. This bill is one step toward ending this cycle of violence."[1]

The animal cruelty law demonstrates how the system of checks and balances works between the legislative, judicial, and executive branches. However, there are other cases where the system does not work. Some critics say that money from lobbyists influences many decisions in the legislature. Sometimes, they argue, legislation that should be passed is not even considered.

One group of important lobbyists represents cable television. Nobody likes paying high prices for cable television, especially for hundreds of channels that subscribers do not watch. Many cable television subscribers would like to switch to what is called a la carte pricing. In this system, subscribers would choose which channels they want and pay for only those channels.

According to critics, the cable television industry employs an army of lobbyists to prevent Congress from even discussing ways to lower cable television bills. The Center for Responsive Politics reported that Comcast, just one of the nation's many cable companies, contributed $2.9 million to political campaigns in the 2009–2010 elections.[2]

Complaints about the power of special interests in government have a long history. Woodrow Wilson, who was U.S. president from 1913 to 1921, denounced the power of big business. He said, "The government,

President Woodrow Wilson pushed important legislation through Congress, including a law that prohibits child labor. In 1917, he asked Congress to declare war on Germany.

which was designed for the people, has got into the hands of their bosses and their employers, the special interests. . . . An invisible empire has been set up above the forms of democracy."[3]

Another story shows how Congress members step into the executive branch's realm at their own peril. The Food and Drug Administration admitted in October of 2010 that it had approved a patch for injured knees manufactured by a company called ReGen Biologics of New Jersey. The FDA said that four congressmen from New Jersey had pressured the agency, which falls under the executive branch, to approve the patch, despite experts' warnings that the patch should not be approved. The four members of Congress—Senators Robert Menendez and Frank R. Lautenberg and Representatives Frank Pallone Jr. and Steven R. Rothman—had all received campaign contributions from ReGen Biologics.[4]

For decades, congressional laws have limited the amount of money businesses may give political candidates. In 2010, the Supreme Court ruled that these laws violated the corporation's right to free speech.[5] Corporate political donations would remain unlimited unless Congress passed a new bill against it.

One of President Obama's major goals as president was to reform the U.S. health care system. He wanted everyone to have affordable access to health care. Two years after he was elected, the Senate and the House of Representatives approved a dramatic reform of the nation's health care system. The new law, which would take effect over several years, would help people get health care while controlling costs. When power in the House of Representatives switched back to the Republicans, many believed the law would be repealed.

"Bill" taught a generation how hard it is to become a law.

# Chapter 5
# A Legislator's Day

In 2007, Nancy Pelosi became the first female Speaker of the House in the history of the United States. Pelosi grew up in Baltimore in a political family; her father was mayor and a member of the House of Representatives. When Pelosi was seventeen, her mother pretended to be ill so that Nancy could have dinner with her father and John F. Kennedy, who would later become president. After graduating from college, Nancy married Paul Pelosi, and the couple eventually moved to San Francisco.

Nancy stayed home to raise their five children while her husband worked in real estate and investing. She volunteered to help with Democratic Party events and soon found herself chair of the Democratic Party of California. In 1987, she was elected to the House of Representatives. Over the years, she has become more and more powerful. During President Barack Obama's first term, she helped him pass new health care legislation and many other important laws.

President Barack Obama embraces
Secretary of Health and Human Services
Kathleen Sebelius, left, and House
Speaker Nancy Pelosi after signing the
health insurance reform bill in 2010.

Nancy Pelosi and Vice President Joe Biden applaud President Obama. The U.S. Constitution lists the vice president's job as presiding over the Senate. Since the vice president is part of the executive branch, a tradition has developed within the Senate that limits the vice president's role. He or she is expected to cast votes only to break ties.

As Speaker of the House, Nancy Pelosi was third in line of succession to the president. In other words, if something had happened to both the president and the vice president, she would have become president. Even though she spends her days meeting and negotiating in the halls of power, she is also a doting grandmother who happily sits on the floor with her grandchildren in the evenings. What else does she do on a typical day?

In one day in 2010, Pelosi sat with President Obama and Vice President Joe Biden at the funeral of Dorothy Height, a pioneer of the civil rights movement. She was also the keynote speaker at the Emily's List fund-raising luncheon. Emily's List raises money for feminist candidates. After the speech, she gave an interview to a magazine writer in which she talked about the importance of electing women to office early. "I want them to gain their **seniority** early on so they can chair committees instead of coming [to Congress] after their children are grown and having to accrue seniority much later in life."[1]

A few hours later she was meeting with a crowd of reporters for her weekly news conference. The reporters followed her down the hall. She smiled at them and then slipped out of sight into her office. Her office is a small empire, with fifty employees spread out over four floors. Her employees study legislation, help constituents who have problems with the federal government, and handle many other questions from voters.

Later in the evening on another one of Pelosi's typical long days, she traveled out of the city to Maryland to speak at a fund-raiser for the

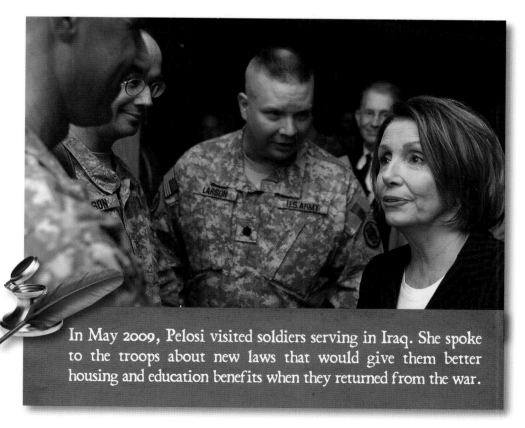

In May 2009, Pelosi visited soldiers serving in Iraq. She spoke to the troops about new laws that would give them better housing and education benefits when they returned from the war.

Democratic Congressional Campaign Committee. The host, Donna Edwards, was the newly elected representative from Maryland's Fourth Congressional District. Edwards is the type of young representative that Pelosi wants to support.

In November 2010, when voters elected a new Republican majority in the House of Representatives, Pelosi lost her position as Speaker of the House. She remained, however, as leader of the Democratic members of the House of Representatives.

"We have no intention of letting our great achievements be rolled back," she wrote in a letter to her fellow Democratic members. "It is my

Republican John Boehner was elected Speaker of the House in November 2010.

Sam Rayburn (right), with President John F. Kennedy (center) and Texas Senator Ralph Yarborough. Rayburn, a Democrat from Bonham, Texas, was Speaker of the House for a total of seventeen years, longer than any Speaker before or since. Many members of the House of Representatives work in the Rayburn House Office Building, which was named in his honor.

hope that we can work in a **bipartisan** way to create jobs and strengthen the middle class."[2]

Pelosi knew that in order to accomplish anything in the new session, the Republican majority would need to work together with the Democratic members of the Congress and the Democratic president. Working across party lines is called bipartisanship.

When the new session of the U.S. Congress opened in 2011, the members began by reading the U.S. Constitution aloud. They wanted to recognize the importance of the document that has guided the U.S. government for so many years. It was an appropriate way to remind the legislators of their solemn duty under a document that has been argued about and amended but remains a strong and enduring framework for our nation's democracy.

## Chapter 1. Democracy in Action

1. Ian Shapira, "A New Breed of Congressman," *Washington Post*, January 7, 2009.
2. Ray Reed, "Hurt Gives Fifth District Back to GOP," *The Daily Progress*, November 2, 2010.

## Chapter 2. The Birth of the U.S. Congress

1. Marjorie G. Fribourg, *The U.S. Congress: Men Who Steered Its Course, 1787–1867* (Philadelphia: Macrae Smith Company, 1972), p. 4.
2. Ibid., p. 9.
3. U.S. Constitution, Article I, Section 9.
4. Fribourg, p. 33.
5. Ibid., p. 36.

## Chapter 3. The Evolution of Congress

1. Robert V. Remini, *The House* (New York: HarperCollins, 2006), p. 41.
2. Marjorie G. Fribourg, *The U.S. Congress: Men Who Steered Its Course, 1787–1867* (Philadelphia: Macrae Smith Company, 1972), p. 68.

## Chapter 4. How a Bill Becomes a Law

1. Lisa Acho Remorenko, "Crush Videos: Animal Snuff Films May Finally Become Illegal," *The Santa Barbara Independent,* July 30, 2010. http://www.independent.com/news/2010/jul/30/crush-videos/

2. "Comcast Corporation," The Center for Responsive Politics, accessed January 10, 2011. http://www.opensecrets.org/orgs/totals.php?cycle=2010&id=D000000461

3. Charles Lewis, *The Buying of Congress* (New York: William Morrow, 1998/2005), p. 7.

4. Gardner Harris, "F.D.A. Vows to Revoke Approval of Device," *The New York Times,* October 14, 2010.

5. Adam Liptak, "Justices, 5-4, Reject Corporate Spending Limit," *The New York Times,* January 21, 2010. http://www.nytimes.com/2010/01/22/us/politics/22scotus.html

## Chapter 5. A Legislator's Day

1. Lynn Sherr, "The Most Powerful Woman in U.S. History," *More,* October 2010, p. 158.

2. "Pelosi to Run for House Minority Leader," *USA Today,* November 5, 2010. http://content.usatoday.com/communities/onpolitics/post/2010/11/nancy-pelosi-to-run-for-house-minority-leader/1

# BOOKS

Fein, Eric. *The U.S. Congress.* Mankato, MN: Capstone Press, 2008.

Jakubiak, David J. *What Does a Congressional Representative Do?* New York: PowerKids Press, 2010.

Jakubiak, David J. *What Does a Senator Do?* New York: PowerKids Press, 2010.

Leavitt, Amie Jane. *Nancy Pelosi.* Hockessin, DE: Mitchell Lane Publishers, 2007.

Taylor-Butler, Christine. *The Congress of the United States.* Danbury, CT: Children's Press, 2008.

# WORKS CONSULTED

The Constitution of the United States
http://www.archives.gov/exhibits/charters/
constitution_transcript.html

Fribourg, Marjorie G. *The U.S. Congress: Men Who Steered Its Course, 1787–1867.* Philadelphia: Macrae Smith Company, 1972.

Harris, Gardner. "F.D.A. Vows to Revoke Approval of Device." *The New York Times,* October 14, 2010.

Lewis, Charles. *The Buying of Congress.* New York: William Morrow, 2005.

Liptak, Adam. "Justices, 5-4, Reject Corporate Spending Limit." *The New York Times,* January 21, 2010. http://www.nytimes.com/2010/01/22/us/politics/22scotus.html

O'Connor, Patrick. "Nancy Pelosi Makes Surprise Visit to Baghdad, Iraq." *Politico,* May 10, 2009. http://www.politico.com/news/stories/0509/22326.html

Packer, George. "The Empty Chamber: Just How Broken Is the Senate?" *The New Yorker,* August 2, 2010.

"Pelosi to Run for House Minority Leader." *USA Today,* November 5, 2010. http://content.usatoday.com/communities/onpolitics/post/2010/11/nancy-pelosi-to-run-for-house-minority-leader/1

Quirk, Paul J., and Sarah A. Binder (editors). *The Legislative Branch.* Oxford: Oxford University Press, 2005.

Reed, Ray. "Hurt Gives Fifth District Back to GOP." *The Daily Progress,* November 2, 2010. Remini, Robert V. *The House.* New York: HarperCollins, 2006.

Remorenko, Lisa Acho. "Crush Videos: Animal Snuff Films May Finally Become Illegal." *The Santa Barbara Independent,* July 30, 2010. http://www.independent.com/news/2010/jul/30/crush-videos/

Ritchie, Donald A. *The Congress of the United States: A Student Companion.* New York: Oxford University Press, 2006.

Shapira, Ian. "A New Breed of Congressman." *Washington Post,* January 7, 2009.

Sherr, Lynn. "The Most Powerful Woman in U.S. History." *More,* October, 2010.

## ON THE INTERNET

The Center for Responsive Politics
http://www.opensecrets.org

The Charters of Freedom: Declaration of Independence, The Constitution, The Bill of Rights
http://www.archives.gov/exhibits/charters/

The Constitution
http://www.whitehouse.gov/our-government/the-constitution

The United States House of Representatives
http://www.house.gov/

The United States Senate
http://www.senate.gov/

The White House
http://www.whitehouse.gov/

**abolish** (uh-BAH-lish)—To do away with; to outlaw.

**amendment** (uh-MEND-munt)—An addition or change to a document.

**bicameral** (by-KAM-uh-rul)—Having two houses or chambers (such as the Senate and the House of Representatives).

**bipartisan** (by-PAR-tih-zin)—Involving two political parties, such as the Democrats and the Republicans.

**copyright** (KAH-pee-ryt)—The legal right to have control over a piece of writing, art, or music.

**counterrevolutionary** (kown-ter-rev-uh-LOO-shuh-nayr-ee)—Having to do with a revolution to overthrow a government that was established by a prior revolution.

**emolument** (ee-MOL-yoo-munt)—A salary, tip, or other advantage or profit gained at a job.

**ex post facto law** (eks pohst FAK-toh law)—A law that tries to punish an activity that took place before the law made that activity a crime.

**habeas corpus** (HAY-bee-us KOR-pus)—A judge's request that a prisoner be brought into court to determine whether the person has been legally imprisoned.

**indict** (in-DYT)—To formally charge someone with a crime.

**infrastructure** (IN-fruh-struk-shur)—The system and resources needed for an activity, such as roads and railroads for transportation.

**lobbyist** (LAH-bee-ist)—A person who is paid to meet with legislators and influence them on behalf of a company, union, or other group.

**midterm election** (MID-term ee-LEK-shun)—An election held two years after the presidential election.

**pardon** (PAR-dun)—To excuse someone of an offense (crime) without making them pay the penalty.

**Quaker** (KWAY-ker)—A member of the Society of Friends, a historically peaceful church with roots in seventeenth-century England.

**ratify** (RAT-ih-fy)—To sign a document to make it official or law.

**seniority** (sen-YOR-ih-tee)—Privilege earned after a length of continuous service.

**speculator** (SPEK-yoo-lay-ter)—A person who buys something with the hope that its value will increase quickly.

**suffrage** (SUF-ridj)—The right to vote.

**Tory** (TOR-ee)—Any of the colonists who sided with Great Britain during the Revolutionary War.

# ABOUT THE
# AUTHOR

Rebecca Thatcher Murcia grew up in Garrison, New York, and graduated from the University of Massachusetts with a double major in Journalism and Social Thought and Political Economy. She worked as a reporter for newspapers in Massachusetts and Texas for fourteen years, and then became a children's book author. Her books for Mitchell Lane Publishers include *The Civil Rights Movement*, *We Visit Colombia*, and a biography of the great inventor Thomas Edison. She lives with her sons in Akron, Pennsylvania. Find out more about the author at http://www.thatchermurcia.com.